Beginning

Moo Duk K

TAE KWON DO

Korean Art of Self-Defense

Volume 1

by Richard Chun, Ph. D
Associate Professor
Hunter College, City University of New York

© Copyright 1975 by Richard Chun

All rights reserved
Printed in the United States of America
Library of Congress Catalog Card Number: 75-3784

Twenty-fifth printing 1999

ISBN 0-89750-015-6

Graphic Design by David Paul Kaplan

WARNING

OHARA PUBLICATIONS, INCORPORATED
SANTA CLARITA, CALIFORNIA

Dr. Un Yong Kim

DEDICATION

To Dr. Un Yong Kim, member of I.O.C., President of the World Tae Kwon Do Federation, the Korea Tae Kwon Do Association and the Kuk Ki Won.

To Grandmaster Chong Soo Hong, Vice-President of the Korea Tae Kwon Do Association and President of the Moo Duk Whe.

ACKNOWLEDGEMENT

I would like to express my deepest appreciation to the following students for their time and effort: Marco A. Vega and Margaret Sauers for their photography, Geraldine Michalik for her editing and Silke Luthge for her drawings.

FOREWORD

Tae kwon do trains both mind and body through strict discipline and places a great emphasis on the development of moral character. Thus, control of the mind over body, patience, kindness, self-restraint, and humility must accompany physical grace. Accordingly, the first thing taught is the bow of respect by which the individual verifies his trust for his teacher and for his friends in practice. By studying the art, the individual comes to understand himself and his opponent. Then he can be silent and fearless. The essence of tae kwon do rests in the integrity of its practitioner.

Tae kwon do, the Korean martial art and Olympic sport, has become increasingly popular in the Western world and is now being practiced by people all over the world as an art of self-defense and also as a competitive sport. At the moment, there are more than 3,000 instructors in some 90 countries abroad who are engaged in teaching the art of tae kwon do.

In 1973, the World Tae Kwon Do Federation, headquartered in Seoul, Korea, was founded through the endless efforts of Un Yong Kim, the president of the Korea Tae Kwon Do Association, for the purpose of promoting and advancing the art of tae kwon do, unifying its members throughout the world and furthering its promotion as an international sport. Moo Duk Kwan, having the prestige of a long history and large membership, is also dedicated to promoting the art of tae kwon do throughout the world.

At the present time in the United States alone, there are more than ten million who practice tae kwon do. This is the first book that has been written to guide and instruct students of Moo Duk Kwan, as well as students who are interested in the art of tae kwon do.

This book covers in detail the principles and philosophical concepts of tae kwon do and Moo Duk Kwan, and is designed to teach all the basic requirements including forms, sparring, and self-defense for white belt through low green belt level. The subsequent book will cover the requirements for intermediate, advanced, and black belt levels.

It is my hope that this book will guide students to the right direction of learning tae kwon do and the principles of Moo Duk Kwan, and will help them achieve a better way of life through physical and spiritual fulfillment.

Richard Chun
New York City

PREFACE

My dear Rhin Moon Richard Chun,

Because there is no place for jealousy in the field of tae kwon do, I can feel only admiration and abundant respect for your latest achievement—specifically, your English edition of Moo Duk Kwan. Long has it been my desire to see such an English version of our revered style of the martial arts. Your fulfillment of this magnanimous undertaking is most gratifying. My congratulations to you from my sincere heart.

Your textbook on Moo Duk Kwan should be of particular interest to the novice practitioner, as well as a re-enforcement for the experienced student and instructor. Your deft explanation of the philosophy as an integral part of the Tae Kwon Do Association is to be commended. Certainly the stress you placed in the area of the philosophy and true understanding of Moo Duk Kwan is of the essence. With due respect for our brethren of the Western culture, it is incumbent upon us to reveal and to interpret the spiritual integrity of this renowned martial art.

Particularly in this day of dwindling respect for authority and for recognized and qualified teachers, we must strive to rekindle the flame of respect among mankind throughout the world. Many must learn and some must re-learn to respect the teacher, especially the Master teacher and his teachings. It is this source from which spiritual appreciation surges. Moo Duk Kwan, as a rejuvenating part of tae kwon do, can lead the way—away from violence, toward mutual respect for all mankind.

The teachers of Moo Duk Kwan have a responsibility toward all students, young and old: the dispensing of self-defense or fighting techniques must go hand in hand with the development of self-control and personal effort, as well as other elements that go into the building of good character. The student need not be a slave for the Master, but should be a disciple of the teachings which the Master seeks to implant. Recognizably, the Master himself must be a glowing example to be emmulated by his followers.

In the world of sport, Moo Duk Kwan has not as yet found its rightful place. Now that the world has been inculcated with the martial arts through various media, it is dependant upon the genuine teacher and student of Moo Duk Kwan to practice and to perform our sport as it should be revealed.

Again, as an art, Moo Duk Kwan can rise to new heights. The movement of body in motion, in balance, in coordination, in meditation, can be a fulfilling, gratifying experience. Moo Duk Kwan, as a glowing element of the Tae Kwon Do Association, can be the avenue upon which the peoples of the world can stroll together in mutual respect and consideration for each other.

I cannot overemphasize the importance of this book to all conscientious students of tae kwon do. Your book has treasures of wisdom and techniques from which all practitioners of our martial art can draw. As you have noted in this day of exploitation and dire misrepresentation of the true idea and ideals of our martial art, we must do all in our power to clarify the true philosophy of Moo Duk Kwan.

I would recommend your book as an outstanding text for anyone interested in knowing about the martial arts as well as for those people who are anxious to learn to practice the art. You have my undying gratitude for the completion of this first English version textbook of Moo Duk Kwan.

Sincerely yours,

Chong Soo Hong
President
Moo Duk Kwan
Seoul, Korea

ABOUT THE AUTHOR

Richard Chun, one of the highest-ranking instructors in tae kwon do in the world, received his ninth dan from the Kuk Ki Won /World Taekwondo Federation. His many impressive credentials include his appointment to the technical committee of the World Taekwondo Federation in 1980, and being named Special Assistant to the President of WTF. He is currently President of the United States Taekwondo Association.

Richard Chun began studying tae kwon do at an early age under Chong Soo Hong in Seoul, Korea, and with Ki Whang Kim. He graduated from Yon Sei University in 1957, where he served as the Team Captain to the Taekwondo Club. He came to the United States in 1962 in order to attend graduate school at the Long Island University in New York. Two years later, he received his M.B.A. degree in Marketing from the School of Business Administration, and his Ph.D. in Education in 1983.

In 1972, Richard Chun was appointed International Master Instructor by the World Taekwondo Federation. Since then he has worked continuously to promote the art and the sport of tae kwon do throughout the world. Chun was head coach for the U.S. team at the First World Taekwondo Championships held in Seoul in 1973, in which the U.S. team took second place. He also served as Technical Director for the Second and the Third World Taekwondo Championships, and in 1979 he was named Instuctor of the Year to *Black Belt* Magazine's Hall of Fame. In addition, he was appointed as an international referee by the World Taekwondo Federation.

Richard Chun has written many articles and features about tae kwon do for various publications, including the books, *Tae Kwon Do—Korean Martial Art,* and *Advancing in Tae Kwon Do*. He has also produced a number of instructional videotapes on the same subject, including *Self-Defense for Women—Fight Back*.

Master Chun maintains his central headquarters in New York City, and has supervised much of the instruction of his art in the United States since 1962.

Dr. Richard Chun is currently an Associate Professor of Physical Education at Hunter College, City University of New York.

Dr. Richard Chun has also been very active in community service to help make his community a better place to live. He has served the New York Jay Cees as Vice-President and as the District Governor of the Lions Club International Association, and the Lions Club's New York District. For his outstanding humanitarian achievements, he has received the highest awards from the Lions Clubs International, and the Presidential Award and medal from the President of Korea.

CONTENTS

DEFINITION OF TAE KWON DO

Literally translated, the Korean word, "tae," means "to kick" or "squash with the foot." "Kwon" implies "a hand or fist to block, punch, strike, or destroy." "Do" denotes an "art" or a "way." Thus, "tae kwon do," means "the art of kicking, blocking and punching."

Tae kwon do is a system of symmetrical body exercises (or a system of techniques) designed for self-defense and counterattack in unarmed combat, making use of the hands and feet as weapons. However, tae kwon do is not merely a physical fighting skill—it is rather, a way of thought and life. Through strict discipline, tae kwon do trains both the mind and body, placing great emphasis on the development of moral character. In other words, control of the mind, self-discipline, kindness and humility must accompany the physical grace.

Tae kwon do training consists of hardening the body through practice of the various attack and defense forms. This system of unarmed combat involves the skillful application of punching, jumping, kicking, dodging, blocking and parrying actions, directed toward the goal of neutralizing an aggressor. Its techniques are essentially linear motions, but also include the use of circular hand movements, throwing and falling techniques. An essential characteristic used in meeting an opponent's attack is the mastery of breathing and the development of *jiptjung* (power gathering) to unify your force.

HISTORY OF TAE KWON DO

There are many theories about the origins of fighting techniques without weapons. The following history is the most traditional view and is believed to be the most credible.

Ancient need for self-protection:

Primitive people, no matter where they lived, had to develop personal fighting skills in order to defend themselves against their enemies. Thus, empty hand fighting did not originate in any one country, but in almost all parts of the globe as it was needed.

As the ancients invented weapons for more effective self-defense and better subsistence, they continued their practice of various games to promote their physical and mental sharpness in the form of religious rites. In Korea's tribal states, many such sporting activities were practiced after the neolithic era. These activities eventually developed into arts to improve health, known today as martial arts. Practitioners imitated the defensive and offensive positions assumed by animals and slowly developed effective skills in hand-to-hand fighting. These gave way to primitive form of *tae-kyon* (an ancient name for tae kwon do).

Development of Korea's tae kwon do:

KOGURYO DYNASTY

The origin of tae kwon do in Korea can be traced back to the Koguryo dynasty, which was founded in 37 B.C. This is evidenced by mural paintings found in the ruins of royal tombs like those of

The ceiling of the Muyong-chong, a royal tomb of the Koguryo Dynasty, bears murals (left and right) of ancient tae kwon do practice. The tomb was excavated in Manchuria by a group of archeologists in 1935 and is believed to have been erected between 3 A.D. and 427 A.D.

Myong-chong and Kak chu-chong in the Hwando province of Manchuria, which depicted figures practicing tae kwon do. The date of these murals seems to indicate that tae kwon do is purely of Korean origin and did not develop as an outgrowth of the Chinese martial art, *kwonbop*, which was introduced to Korea in 520 A.D.

SILLA DYNASTY

Silla was a kingdom founded in the southeastern part of Korea some twenty years before Koguryo. In Kyong ju, the ancient capital of Silla, there are two Buddhist images inscribed on the Keum Kang Giant Tower that face one another in a tae kwon do stance.

Silla is also famous for its Hwarang-do, the knights errant who devoted themselves to hunting, learning and the martial arts. Development of the martial arts was an essential part of Silla's struggle to unify the whole country, as tae kwon do played a major part in the physical training of the Hwarang-do.

KORYO DYNASTY

Founded in 918 A.D., the Koryo dynasty picked up the martial arts gauntlet from its predecessors and elevated it to great popularity among its common people. Records indicate that the Koryo dynasty practiced tae kwon do (termed *subak* at that time) as a martial art as well as a sporting activity.

YI DYNASTY

During the Yi dynasty, a book was written to teach tae kwon do as a martial art rather than a game. This step ended the monopoly which the military society exercised on subak and gave it to the public.

In the latter part of the Yi dynasty, subak's importance as a martial art declined, but it retained its popularity as recreation for the common people. The subsequent occupation of Korea by Japan during the early 1900's saw an end of the Yi dynasty and a temporary restriction of martial arts practice.

TWENTIETH CENTURY

Between the period of Japanese occupation and the Korean War (i.e., from the turn of the century through 1950) the terminology for the Korean martial art changed several times. It was known as *kong soo* (empty hand), *tang soo* (tang hand), and *hwa soo* (hwarang hand) until the title tae kwon do was officially adopted in 1955.

On May 16, 1961, the "Tae Soo Do Association" was formed to unite the various similar systems which existed in Korea at that time. On February 23, 1963, the Association joined the Korean Athletic Association and began to participate in national tournaments. By 1965, the name was changed again to the "Korean Tae Kwon Do Association" with Young Chai Kim as its elected president.

In 1970, the Board of Directors of the Tae Kwon Do Association elected Master Un Yong Kim as their next president. Since that time, his many efforts and contributions have helped tae kwon do flourish and spread in popularity to become the national sport of Korea. Tae kwon do is now included as part of the school curriculum from the first grade through college and is a requisite for military training.

In 1972, Master Un Yong Kim was elected president of Kuk Ki Won, the National Central Gymnasium which was built in Seoul to train advanced students. Kuk Ki Won provides a testing center for black belt promotions, serves as a research center for the advancement of tae kwon do as a scientific sport, and is used to hold national and international tae kwon do championship tournaments.

In May 1973, the first World Tae Kwon Do Championship was held at Kuk Ki Won, Seoul, Korea, in which approximately 30 countries participated. In team competition, Korea won first place, the United States won second place, and Mexico and the Republic of China tied for third place. The World Championship is held bi-annually.

Following the tournament, all the officials representing their countries at the championship formed the World Tae Kwon Do Federation in May, 1973, and voted Master Un Yong Kim as president.

Tae kwon do was introduced to the United States during the latter part of the 1950s and has since spread in popularity. In May, 1974, tae kwon do was officially recognized as a sport in the United States and was accepted as a member of the AAU (Amateur Athletic Union), subsequently becoming a member of U.S. Olympic Committee.

In May, 1981, with the untiring efforts of Dr. Un Yong Kim, the IOC approved the inclusion of tae kwon do in the 1988 Olympic Games, Seoul, Korea, as a demonstration game.

In 1982, Dr. Un Yong Kim was elected as a member of the IOC. Since then, he has been serving on the IOC Executive Board as an executive member.

During the 1988 Olympic Games, tae kwon do was voted to be included in the 1992 Olympic Games to be held in Spain, as a demonstration game again. It hopes to participate in the 1996 Olympic Games as an official sport.

HISTORY OF MOO DUK KWAN

Moo Duk Kwan, translated literally means "the institute of martial virtue." It was founded in Seoul, Korea, by Hwang Kee on November 6, 1945, following World War II (Korea was liberated from Japan on August 15, 1945). In that same year, Hwang Kee became the first president of the Moo Duk Kwan. Moo Duk Kwan was able to develop and expand its branch schools and members through his endless efforts and contributions.

Hwang Kee formed the Korea Tang Soo Do Association in September, 1953, and Moo Duk Kwan became a member of the Korea Tang Soo Do Association. In December, 1953, the Korea Tang Soo Do Association unsuccessfully tried to join the Korean Athletic Association. In June, 1960, the Korean Soo Bahk Do Association, named after the traditional Korean martial art, was formed by Hwang to replace the Korean Tang Soo Do Association. The Tang Soo Do Association was liquidated, and Moo Duk Kwan subsequently became a member of the Soo Bahk Do Association.

In March, 1965, the Soo Bahk Do Association attempted to unite with the Korea Tae Kwon Do Association, but the effort was unsuccessful.

After the failure, a majority of the Moo Duk Kwan members left the Soo Bahk Do Association and joined the Korea Tae Kwon Do Association.

In April, 1965, Moo Duk Kwan officially became a member of the Korea Tae Kwon Do Association. On November 20, 1965, Master Kang Ik Lee was elected by the Board of Directors of the Moo Duk Kwan as the president of Moo Duk Kwan, Korea Tae Kwon Do Association. Unfortunately, Moo Duk Kwan was now divided into the Tae Kwon Do Association and the Soo Bahk Do Association. On July 27, 1971, the Board of Directors of Moo Duk Kwan elected Master Chong Soo Hong as the third President of the Moo Duk Kwan, Tae Kwon Do Association. Several attempts were made by Master Chong Soo Hong to unify the two divided Moo Duk Kwans, but his efforts have not yet been successful.

In February, 1974, however, as a result of Master Hong's contributions to tae kwon do, he was appointed Vice-President of the Tae Kwon Do Central Gymnasium (Kuk Ki Won) in Seoul, Korea.

In 1989, Master Hong was appointed Vice-President of the Korea Tae Kwon Do Association, Seoul, Korea.

THE PHILOSOPHY OF
TAE KWON DO

The philosophy of martial arts as applied in tae kwon do is based on the unity of spirit with physical action. In order to effectively act as a natural weapon in a given moment, the body's muscles and joints must be trained to coordinate movement. However, the development of the body and the coordination of tae kwon do techniques are not fully effective unless they occur in conjunction with the training of moral character, kindness, self-discipline, patience, forgiveness, and humility.

Thus, meditation is practiced to unify the body and mind; thoughts are clarified and actions made more efficient. Knowing (that is understanding that the individual is complete within) provides the ability to act confidently. Concentration also contributes toward achieving optimum performance; as does a sense of calm and determination which overcomes distraction and troubled perception. Life is enriched.

The application of the yin and yang principles further allows certain areas of the body to be utilized to their maximum potential. The yin and yang or the soft and hard areas of the body are trained to react with speed and agility in appropriate ways. The soft areas of the body for instance, are pliable and are not used to resist attack. They are used to allow the opponent to be carried off balance. The hard areas of the body being resistant, are used to fend off the attacker. When applied correctly, the principles of yin and yang place the opponent at a disadvantage.

The individual must realize that to defend one's life means also to risk losing it and by accepting such a likelihood, fear will not cause distraction. The trained mind and body acting in unison is like intuitive reflex. The body's response is synchronized with perception.

Tae kwon do is a combination of a state of mind working in unison with a trained body. When kindness and humility accompany physical grace the use of tae kwon do becomes an art. Unlike the Western idea of technique and proficiency in skills as the ultimate goal in defensive development, the Eastern idea goes beyond such limits and incorpporates the martial art as a way of being one with the world. Consciously living in harmonious unison with all there is around you on a daily basis is the philosophy of tae kwon do in action, not the use of the body as a destructive tool for wanton purposes. What is learned in tae kwon do is the ability to distinguish necessary from unnecessary antagonisms in the cause of self preservation, not the wasting of energies in fear and destruction.

The individual overcomes his lack of faith in himself through the development of bodily skills and natural strengths in conjunction with a sense of oneness; and the ultimate goal, to live, is achieved.

ASPECTS OF MOO DUK KWAN

MOO DUK KWAN PRINCIPLES

1. Responsibility
2. Sincerity
3. Justice

---

10 CREEDS OF MOO DUK KWAN

1. Be loyal to your country.
2. Be obedient to your parents.
3. Be loveable between husband and wife.
4. Be cooperative between brothers.
5. Be respectful to your elders.
6. Be faithful between teacher and student.
7. Be faithful between friends.
8. Be just in killing.
9. Never retreat in battle.
10. Accompany your decisions with action and always finish what you start.

---

11 POINTS OF EMPHASIS ON MENTAL TRAINING

1. Reverence for nature.
2. Physical concentration (Ki-up).
3. Courtesy.
4. Modesty.
5. Thankfullness
6. Self-sacrifice.
7. Cultivate courage.
8. Chastity.
9. Be strong inside and mild outside.
10. Endurance.
11. Reading ability.

10 POINTS OF EMPHASIS ON PHYSICAL DEVELOPMENT

1. Vocal exhalation, for thoractic strength. (KI-UP).
2. Focus of sight.
3. Continuous balance during movements.
4. Flexibility of the body.
5. Correct muscle tone for maximum power.
6. High and low speed techniques.
7. Exactness of techniques.
8. Adjustment for proper distance.
9. Proper breathing for endurance.
10. Conditioning hands and feet.

---

5 REQUISITES ON MENTAL TRAINING

1. Oneness with nature.
2. Complete awareness of environment.
3. Experience.
4. Conscience.
5. Culture.

MATTERS THAT DEMAND SPECIAL ATTENTION WHILE TRAINING IN MOO DUK KWAN

1. Purpose of training should be enhancement of the mental and physical self.
2. Sincerity is necessary.
3. Effort is necessary.
4. Consistent schedule during practice.
5. Do your best when training.
6. Train in the basic spirit of Moo Duk Kwan.
7. Regularly spaced practice sessions.
8. Obey without objection the word of instructors or seniors; look and learn.
9. Don't be overly ambitious.
10. Pay attention to every aspect of your training.
11. Pay attention to the order of training.
12. Get instruction step by step in new forms and techniques.
13. Try to conquer when you feel idleness.
14. Cleanliness is desired after practice is finished.

KOREAN FLAG

The flag of "Tae Kook" is the Korean flag. "Tae Kook" means "the origin of all things in the universe." The circle in the center of the flag is divided into portions of red and blue by a horizontal "S." These red and blue portions symbolize the Um and Yang theory of eternal duality which exists within nature (e.g., heaven and earth; light and darkness; hot and cold; being and not being). In science, this theory can be represented with the symbols "+" and "-". These dualities exist as a principle of the universe.

The four "Gye" (bar designs), in the corners of the flag, are based on the Um and Yang principle of light and darkness. The location of these Gye represent the four points of the compass. Ee-Gye in the lower left corner, indicates dawn and early sunlight as the sun rises in the east. Kun-Gye, in the upper left, represents bright sunshine when the sun is in the south. Kam-Gye in the upper right corner symbolizes twilight as the sun moves to the west. Kon-Gye in the lower right, indicates total darkness when the sun is in the north. Together these symbols express the mysteries of the universe.

MOO DUK KWAN EMBLEM

1. Laurel leaves—The fourteen laurel leaves on each side, represent the fourteen states of Korea and the advancement of peace.
2. The three seeds joined to the laurel leaves on each side of the emblem represent the "three thousand Li" (the distance running north to south) of the "Land of Morning Calm" and its success.
3. The six seeds in total indicate the world and represent the six continents.
4. The fist represents tae kwon do and justice.
5. The Korean character in the center of the circle means Moo Duk Kwan.
6. The character on the left of the circle means tae and the character on the right of the circle means kwon.
7. The deep blue color of the emblem represents the three oceans and black belts.

As a whole, the emblem symbolizes the spreading of Moo Duk Kwan throughout the fourteen states, i.e., all of Korea, and then across the oceans to the six continents of the world. Moo Duk Kwan, as an international institution, is to achieve the objectives of peace and human advancement as the emblem symbolizes.

BASIC STRIKING WEAPONS

The effectiveness of tae kwon do techniques lies in developing maximum concentration of power and speed in order to utilize hard areas of the body as striking weapons for defense and attacking purposes. There are numerous hard surfaces of the body which could be used as weapons. It is equally important to know the vital points which are the weakest parts of the body in order to deliver an effective attack. This book covers the basic weapons which will be most useful to the beginning student.

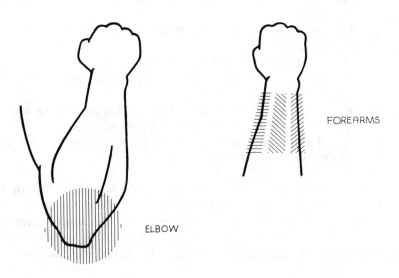

FOREARMS

ELBOW

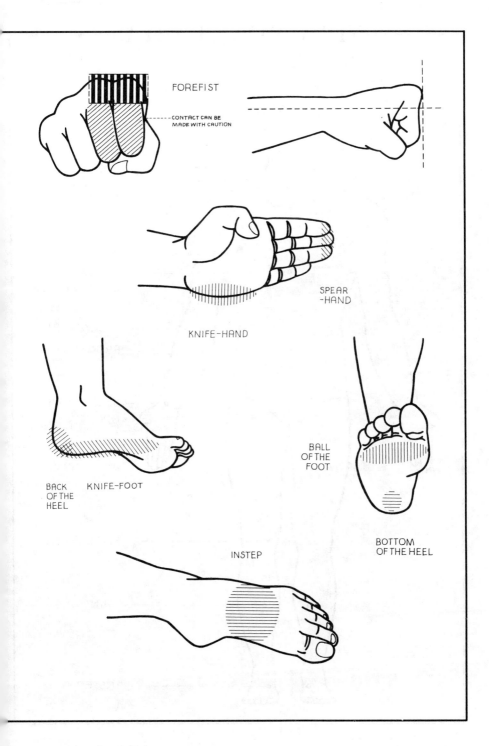

FOREFIST

CONTACT CAN BE
MADE WITH CAUTION

SPEAR-HAND

KNIFE-HAND

BACK OF THE HEEL

KNIFE-FOOT

BALL OF THE FOOT

BOTTOM OF THE HEEL

INSTEP

VITAL TARGET AREAS

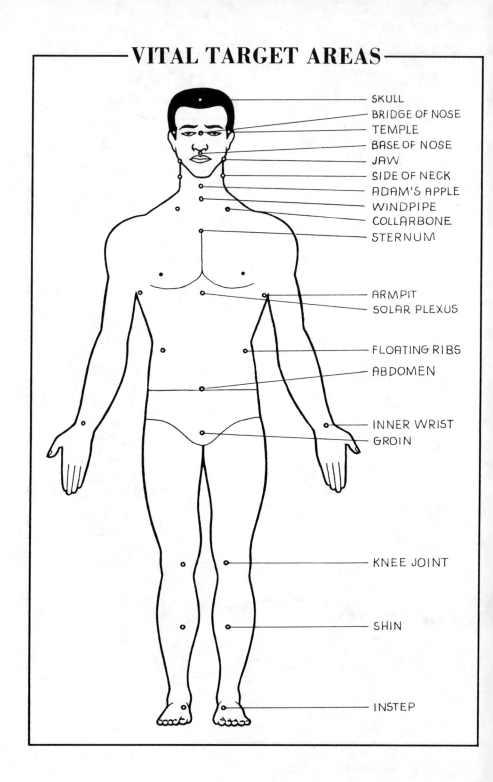

SKULL
BRIDGE OF NOSE
TEMPLE
BASE OF NOSE
JAW
SIDE OF NECK
ADAM'S APPLE
WINDPIPE
COLLARBONE
STERNUM

ARMPIT
SOLAR PLEXUS

FLOATING RIBS

ABDOMEN

INNER WRIST
GROIN

KNEE JOINT

SHIN

INSTEP

VITAL TARGET AREAS

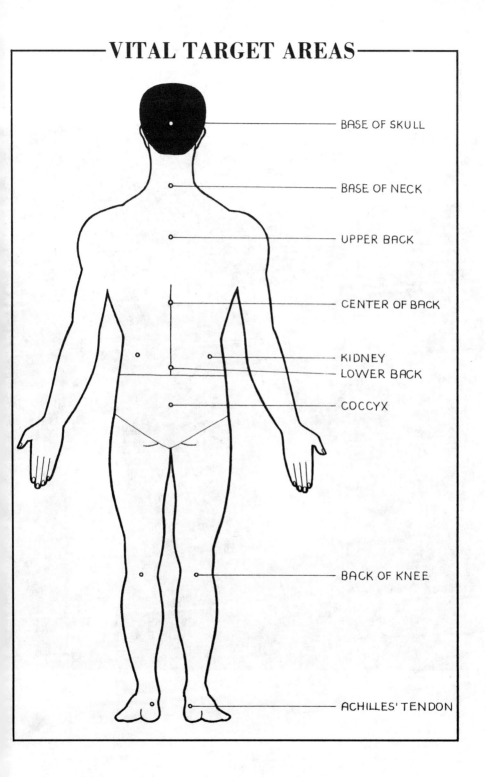

BASE OF SKULL

BASE OF NECK

UPPER BACK

CENTER OF BACK

KIDNEY
LOWER BACK

COCCYX

BACK OF KNEE

ACHILLES' TENDON

WARM-UP EXERCISES

The practice of tae kwon do requires that the body be limber and strong in order to avoid injury and to perform techniques effectively. Warm-up exercises are thus important because they relax the mind and develop a sense of confidence through flexibility and control of the body. There are many exercises used in the practice of tae kwon do, such as those for the neck, shoulder, sides, back, hip, arms, fingers, legs, etc. However, since tae kwon do emphasizes kicking techniques, this book provides examples of those stretching exercises which will help the beginning student develop kicking techniques.

The training schedule should include a variety of exercises for loosening and strengthening the muscles, such as jumping and running, sit-ups, leg raises, and push-ups. It is also important to refresh the body by breathing properly from time to time. This is done by inhaling deeply through the nose and exhaling air completely through the mouth.

SIDE STRETCH

(1) Stand erect with your feet approximately a shoulder width apart, your left hand at your waist and your right hand held upward to shoulder level. From here, bend your body down to the left at the waist. Return to the original position and repeat this exercise seven or eight times. (2) Stand erect with your feet approximately a shoulder width apart, your right hand at your waist and your left hand held upward to shoulder level. From here, bend your body down to the right at the waist, and then return to the original position. Repeat this exercise seven or eight times.

LEG STRETCH

(1) Stand erect on your left leg while grasping the heel of your right foot with your right hand. (2) Lift your right hand upward, extending your right leg in its grasp until the leg is fully extended as high as possible. Repeat this exercise using the other leg and hand.

PUSH-UPS

Assume the normal push-up position and execute the exercise the desired number of times. It would be best to begin with your full open hands making contact with the floor and your feet together, but as you gain proficiency, you may incorporate push-ups on your knuckles with your legs crossed over one another, or on your ten fingertips, or simply on four fingertips (as seen in the illustration).

SIDE SPLIT NO. 1

(1) Begin by sitting on the floor with your legs spread apart as far as possible, your knees locked and your toes pointed upward. Place your left hand behind your head and bend your upper body to the right until your forehead touches your knee. (2) Raise your torso while placing your right hand behind your head and bend to the left until your forehead touches your left knee.

SIDE SPLIT NO. 2

(1) Begin by sitting on the floor with your legs spread apart as far as possible with your knees locked and your toes pointing upward. Grasp your toes with both hands and bend your upper body forward until your forehead touches the floor.

FRONT KICK STRETCH

(1) Extend your right leg forward and rest its heel on the shoulder of your partner. (Beginners may find it easier to have their partner squatting at this point.) Have your partner grasp your extended leg at the ankle with both hands as he slowly rises to his full height. From here, lean your upper torso forward until your forehead touches your knee. Repeat this exercise using your other leg.

SIDE KICK STRETCH

(1) Extend your left leg out sideward and rest its inside ankle on the shoulder of your partner. (Beginners may find it easier to have their partner squatting at this point.) Have your partner grasp your extended leg with both hands as he slowly rises to his full height. (2) Bend your upper body downward in the opposite direction of your extended leg. Repeat this exercise using your other leg.

BASIC STANCES

To insure correct technique, it is essential that you learn the following stances correctly with perfect balance. This volume covers the four basic stances which are necessary for the beginner. They are: the ready stance, the horseback stance (or straddle leg stance), the front stance (or forward stance), and the back stance.

READY STANCE (Choon-Bi-So-Ki)

Stand erect with your feet parallel and a shoulder width apart. Your toes should be pointing straight ahead and your knees should be locked. Hold both of your fists tensely in front of your abdomen, approximately one fist-length forward of your abdomen. Be sure to look straight ahead and pull your jaw inward.

HORSEBACK STANCE
(Ju-Choom-So-Ki)

Stand erect with your feet parallel
and about two shoulders-width apart.
Your toes should be pointing straight
ahead with your knees bent forward.
Hold both of your fists tense at your
hips with the palms upward. Look
straight ahead and pull your jaw
inward.

WALKING IN THE HORSEBACK STANCE

(1) Begin by assuming a horseback stance with your right foot forward. (2) Pivot clockwise on the ball of your right foot and slide your left foot forward until it is parallel and close to your right foot. (3) Continue pivoting on the ball of your right foot as you slide your left foot forward into another horseback stance.

WALKING IN THE FRONT STANCE

(1) Assume a left front stance. (2 & 3) Slide your right foot forward in an arc past your left foot into a right front stance. Your waist should remain almost level during this movement.
Continue stepping both forward and backward.

FRONT STANCE (Ap-Kubi)

Place your feet a shoulder width apart, one foot one and a half steps in front of the other, with your

weight on your forward leg. Your forward knee is above your toe, both pointed straight ahead. Lock your rear leg with that foot pointing 45 degrees to the outside.

TURNING IN THE FRONT STANCE

(1) Assume a left front stance. (2) Slide your rear foot straight across and behind you, a shoulder width from your left foot. (3) Pivot clockwise on the balls of your feet until you achieve a right front stance. Shift your weight primarily to your forward foot.
Practice turning in both directions.

2

3

2

3

WALKING IN THE BACK STANCE

(1) Assume a left back stance (left foot forward). (2 & 3) Slide your rear foot forward, pivoting on the ball of your left foot into a right back stance. Repeat walking forward slowly, then at walking pace. Practice walking backward.

BACK STANCE (Dui-Kubi)

Place one foot in front of the other, one step apart and 90 degrees to each other. Bend your rear leg and center two thirds of your weight above that

foot. Bend your front leg slightly with that heel directly in front of your rear heel. Your chest faces the direction of your rear foot and your head faces the direction of your front foot.

TURNING IN THE BACK STANCE

(1) Assume a left back stance. (2) Pivot your left heel 90 degrees so it is parallel with your right foot, then begin sliding your right foot outward, slightly to the side, while turning it 90 degrees clockwise. (3) Shift your weight back into a right back stance.

1

1

2

3

2

3

PUNCHING TECHNIQUES
(Chu-Mok-Ji-Lu-Ki)

In developing an effective attack, one must learn to strike with various parts of the body. Depending upon the opponent's size and distance from you, correct techniques must be applied as well. This section covers those techniques which are most basic, i.e., the straight punch, the reverse punch and the side punch. Knife hand strikes, elbow strikes, kicking techniques and knee thrusts will be covered in later chapters.

It is important to deliver a punch correctly so that speed, accuracy and power can be obtained without injury to your hand. The straight punch is normally practiced in the horseback stance and usually has the face, shin, neck, solar plexus, abdomen or kidney as its target.

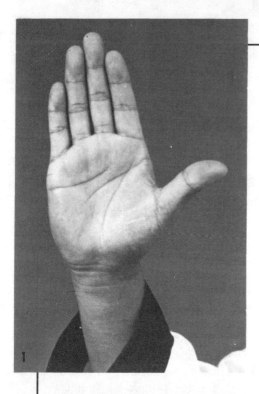

HOW TO MAKE A FIST

(1) Begin by opening your hand with all of your fingers extended. (2) Bend your top four fingers downward toward your palm while leaving your thumb extended. (3) Curl your

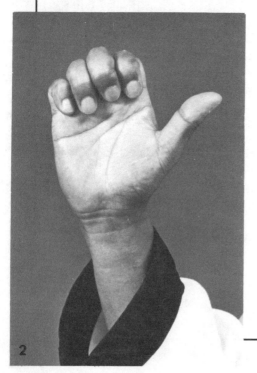

four fingertips into the center of your palm and clench them together tightly. (4) Press your thumb tightly against your index and middle fingers between the second and third knuckles.

STRAIGHT PUNCH
(Ju-Choom-So-Ki-Ji-Lu-Ki)

(1) Begin by assuming a horseback stance with both fists extended in front of your abdomen. (2) Bring both fists to your hips, holding your palms upward. (3 & 4) Punch forward with your right fist, being sure to twist the palm downward as it approaches to one third of the distance to the target. (5) Begin punching forward with your left fist while you simultaneously retract your right fist to your hip. (6) Complete the left straight punch with your left palm downward. The completion of the punch should coincide with the retraction of your right fist to your hip with the palm upward.

When punching, apply coordination first for speed and then concentrate on power and accuracy.

APPLICATION

WALKING STRAIGHT PUNCH
(Ba-Ro-Ji-Lu-Ki)

(1) Begin by assuming the ready stance. (2 & 3) Slide your left foot forward until you achieve a left front stance and simultaneously execute a left straight punch. Be sure to turn your punching fist palm downward and retract your other fist to your hip, palm upward. (4 & 5) Slide your right foot past your left until you have achieved a right front stance and simultaneously execute a right straight punch while retracting your left fist to your hip.

Practice this technique aiming your punches at stomach level and then concentrate on face and groin levels. Following this, you may practice with single, double, or triple punches on each step.

2

4

5

TURNING STRAIGHT PUNCH

(1) Begin by assuming a right front stance. (2) Execute a 180-degree clockwise turn (see front stance turning in previous section) and cock your left arm across your right shoulder. (3) Complete the turn by sliding into a left front stance and simultaneously execute a left low block by swinging your left fist

outward until it is above your left knee. Be sure to retract your right fist to your hip at the same time. (4) Slide your right foot past your left until you achieve a right front stance and simultaneously execute a right straight punch. Remember to retract your left fist to your hip at the same time.

WALKING REVERSE PUNCH
(Ban-De-Ji-Lu-Ki)

(1) Begin by assuming a ready stance. (2 & 3) Slide your left foot forward into a left front stance and simultaneously execute a right reverse punch (the same as you would execute a straight punch). Be sure to retract your left fist to your hip while doing this. (4 & 5) Slide your right foot past your left until you achieve a right front stance and simultaneously execute a left reverse punch.

The reverse punch is applied the same way as the straight punch except that you are punching with the hand on the same side as your rear foot. This punch is most effective as a counterattack after blocking an attack. It can be applied in both the front and back stances.

NOTE: In Korean terminology, "walking punch" means what is seen here as a reverse punch (i.e., punching with the fist that is opposite of the leg that happens to be forward), and reverse punch means what is seen here as a walking punch. To avoid confusion, Western terminology will be used in this book. However, the reader should be aware of this discrepancy.

2

3

5

APPLICATION

TURNING REVERSE PUNCH

(1) Begin by assuming a right front stance. (2) Execute a 180-degree clockwise turn and cock your left arm across your right shoulder. (3) As you slide into a left front stance, execute a left low block by swinging your left fist outward until it is above your knee. (4) From the same stance, execute a right reverse punch while retracting your left fist to your hip.

SIDE PUNCH
(Yop-Ji-Lu-Ki)

The side punch is usually applied from the horseback stance (as seen in the application) because weight distribution is equal on both legs, thus allowing freedom of motion in either direction. The side punch is directly out to the left or right side of your body with the punching arm extended at shoulder level. It is similar to the straight punch in that the punching arm moves straight out and the palm turns downward upon completion of the punch. Both shoulders should be in a straight line with the punching arm and the opposite hand should be retracted to the hip with its palm pointed upward.

WALKING SIDE PUNCH

(1) Begin by assuming the ready stance. (2 & 3) Slide your left foot forward into a horseback stance while you simultaneously execute a left side punch. (4 & 5) Slide your right foot past your left into a horseback stance which has your chest facing in the opposite direction and simultaneously execute a right side punch.

1

3

2

4

5

TURNING SIDE PUNCH

(1) Begin by assuming a horseback stance and a right side punch posture. (2) Slide your left foot in toward your right while you simultaneously turn your upper torso until

your right fist points over your left foot. (3) Step out again with your left foot into a horseback stance and simultaneously execute a left side punch.

BLOCKING TECHNIQUES
(Mak-Ki)

Since tae kwon do is designed for unarmed self-defense, great emphasis should be placed on blocking techniques before going on to more advanced attacks. If the block is properly applied, it can not only be used for defensive purposes, but also can break an opponent's balance as a preliminary to a counterattack.

This chapter deals only with the three most basic blocks, the low, high and middle block (the latter being covered in both inside to outside and outside to inside motions). The knife hand block will be covered in a later chapter.

The blocking surface for the high and low block is the outer edge of your forearm. The middle block, inside to outside, uses the inner edge of your forearm while the outer edge is used when blocking in the opposite direction.

LOW BLOCK
(A-Le-Mak-Ki)

(1) Begin by holding your blocking arm across your chest and above your shoulder with your forearm at a 45-degree angle to the floor. The elbow of your blocking arm should be pointed down toward the floor while your fist should be held palm upward. Your opposite arm should be held horizontally across your abdomen with the palm downward. (2) To initiate the block, sweep your blocking arm across your chest with the palm of your fist beginning to turn downward. It should pass close

to your opposite arm which is simultaneously being retracted toward your hip with its palm turning upward. (3) To complete the block, fully extend your blocking arm a few inches in front of your hip with the palm of its fist turned downward. Your other arm should be fully retracted to your lowest rib with the palm upward. The blocking surface should be the outer edge of your forearm.

NOTE: This low block is normally applied in the front stance, as seen in the application.

APPLICATION

61

WALKING LOW BLOCK

(1) Begin by assuming a ready stance. (2) Move your left foot forward while you fold your arms across your chest in preparation for a low block (see step 1 of low block). (3) Lean forward and assume a left front stance while you simultaneously execute a left low block. (4 & 5) Slide your right foot past your left into a right front stance and execute a right low block. Be sure to fold your arms during the step so that the block may be executed with the completion of the stance.

Practice moving forward with alternate steps and blocks and then practice moving backward with the low block.

2

4

5

TURNING
WITH LOW BLOCK

(1) Begin by assuming a right front stance in a right low block posture. (2 & 3) Make a 180-degree counter-

clockwise turn into a left front stance (see previous stance turning section) and simultaneously execute a left low block.

HIGH BLOCK
(Ol-Gool-Mak-Ki)

(1) Begin by holding your blocking arm across your abdomen and close to your body with its palm turned upward. Your opposite arm should cross your chest with the palm down and the fist placed in front of your shoulder. (2) To initiate the block, swing your blocking arm upward and to the outside of your other arm, crossing it at chest level with the palm turning away from you. Your opposite arm should simultaneously begin its retraction to the hip with the palm turning up-

2

ward. (3) To complete the block, bend your blocking arm so that it shields your face, level with your forehead at about two fists distance. The palm should be pointing away from you and your forearm should be at a 45-degree angle to the floor. Your opposite arm should be simultaneously retracted to your lowest rib with the palm upward. The blocking surface is the outer edge of your forearm.

NOTE: The high block is normally applied in the front stance, as seen in the application.

APPLICATION

3

67

WALKING HIGH BLOCK

(1) Begin by assuming a ready stance. (2 & 3) Slide your left foot forward into a left front stance while you simultaneously execute a left high block. (4 & 5) Slide your right foot past your left into a right front stance and execute a right high block. Be sure to cock your arms during the step so that the block is executed with the completion of the stance.

Practice moving forward with alternate steps and blocks and then practice moving backward with this block.

68

5

TURNING
WITH HIGH BLOCK

(1) Begin by assuming a right front stance in a right high block posture. (2 & 3) Make a 180-degree counter-

clockwise turn into a left front stance and simultaneously execute a left high block.

MIDDLE BLOCK INSIDE TO OUTSIDE
(Mom-Tong-Pakat-Mak-Ki)

(1) Begin by holding your blocking arm across your abdomen, palm downward with the forearm parallel to the floor. Your opposite arm should be held across your chest at shoulder level, parallel above your blocking arm with its palm downward. (2) To initiate the block, swing your blocking arm upward and to the outside of your other arm, crossing it at chest level with the palm turning inward. Your opposite arm should simultaneously begin retracting to your hip with its palm turning upward. (3) To complete the block, swing your blocking arm to the outside so that your fist

is level and in a straight line with your shoulders. The palm of your blocking arm should be pointed toward you while your elbow points to the floor and your forearm is at a 45-degree angle to the floor. The fist of your opposite arm should simultaneously be retracted to your lowest rib with the palm upward. The blocking surface is the inner edge of your forearm.

By raising this block to shoulder level, it can also be used as defense against attack to the face.

NOTE: This middle block is normally applied in the front stance or in the back stance as seen in the application.

APPLICATION

WALKING MIDDLE BLOCK—INSIDE TO OUTSIDE

(1) Begin by assuming a ready stance. (2 & 3) Slide your left foot forward into a left back stance, or (4) a left front stance, and simultaneously execute a left inside to outside middle block. (5 & 6) Slide your right foot past your left into a right back stance or (7) a right front stance, and simultaneously execute a right inside to outside middle block. Be sure to cock your arms during the step so that the block may be executed with the completion of the stance.

Practice moving forward with alternate steps and blocks and then practice moving backward with this block.

1

4

5

2

3

6

7

TURNING WITH INSIDE
TO OUTSIDE MIDDLE BLOCK

(1) Begin by assuming a right back
stance in a right inside to outside
middle block posture. (2 & 3) Make a
180-degree counterclockwise turn

into a left back stance (see previous stance turning section) and simultaneously execute a left inside to outside middle block.

MIDDLE BLOCK OUTSIDE TO INSIDE
(Mom-Tong-Ahn-Mak-Ki)

(1) Begin by holding your blocking arm out to the side with your elbow level to the shoulder and your forearm at a 90-degree angle to the floor. Keep your wrist straight and your palm facing away from you. Your opposite arm should be extended in front of you with its palm downward. (2) To initiate the block, sweep your blocking arm downward and across your chest with your palm turning inward. Your opposite arm should simultaneously begin retracting toward your hip with its palm turning upward. (3) To complete the

block, bring your blocking arm across your chest until its fist is level with your opposite shoulder. The palm should be facing inward with the forearm at a 45-degree angle to the floor. The fist of your opposite arm should simultaneously be retracted to your lowest rib with the palm upward. The blocking surface is the outer edge of your forearm. By raising this block to shoulder level, it can also be used as defense against attack to the face.

NOTE: This middle block is normally applied in the front stance, or in the back stance as seen in the application.

APPLICATION

WALKING
MIDDLE BLOCK—OUTSIDE
TO INSIDE

(1) Begin by assuming a ready stance. (2 & 3) Slide your left foot forward into a left back stance, or (4) a left front stance, and simultaneously execute a left outside to inside middle block. (5 & 6) Slide your right foot past your left into a right back stance or (7) a right front stance and simultaneously execute a right outside to inside middle block. Be sure to cock your arms during the step so that the block may be executed with the completion of the stance.

Practice moving forward with alternate steps and blocks and then practice moving backward with this block.

1

4

5

2

3

6

7

TURNING WITH OUTSIDE
TO INSIDE MIDDLE BLOCK

(1) Begin by assuming a right back stance in a right outside to inside middle block posture. (2 & 3) Make a

180-degree counterclockwise turn into a left back stance and simultaneously execute a left outside to inside middle block.

KNIFE AND SPEAR HAND BLOCKS AND ATTACKS (Sohn-Nal, Sohn-Koot)

Knife hand techniques can be used in both blocking and striking, because the striking edge of the knife hand is sharp and can inflict damage in the performance of both techniques. The sharp striking surface involves the outer ridge of the hand.

The spear hand is used mainly for penetration with its usual targets being the ribs, solar plexus, throat and groin. Its striking surface involves the tips of your three middle fingers.

Both the knife hand and spear hand are formed in the same way, their principle difference being in their striking surfaces. To form a knife hand and spear hand, you should first squeeze your four fingers together while keeping them extended. Following this, bend the three longer fingers slightly downward while you press inward with your pinkie and index fingers. Bend your thumb down into the inside of your palm to complete this formation.

KNIFE HAND MIDDLE BLOCK
(Sohn-Nal-Momtong-Makki)

(1) Begin by holding your blocking arm across your chest with your knife hand resting near the front of your opposite shoulder, palm inward. Pull your opposite arm back so that its knife hand is even with your waist, palm downward. (2) To initiate the block, swing your blocking arm outward across your chest, twisting your palm outward. Your opposite arm should simultaneously begin moving forward with its palm twisting upward. (3) To complete the block, swing your blocking hand outward until its fingertips are even with your shoulder, palm downward. Your opposite arm should lie across your abdomen, palm upward, with the forearm parallel to the floor. Both wrists and arms should tense upon contact.

APPLICATION

KNIFE HAND LOW BLOCK (Sohn-Nal-Ale-Makki)

This block is executed in the same manner as the first two steps of the knife hand middle block. The third step differs in that your blocking arm sweeps down with a low block, palm downward and about two fists distance above the knee, as seen in the application.

KNIFE HAND HIGH BLOCK (Sohn-Nal-Olgool-Makki)

This block is executed in the same manner as the first two steps of the knife hand middle block. The third step differs in that your blocking arm sweeps upward with your fingertips at forehead level and the palm facing away from you, as seen in the application.

WALKING KNIFE
HAND MIDDLE BLOCK

(1) Begin by assuming a ready stance.
(2 & 3) Slide your left foot forward
into a left back stance and simultaneously execute a left knife hand
middle block. (4 & 5) Slide your
right foot past your left into a right
back stance and simultaneously execute a right knife hand middle block.
Be sure to cock your arm during the
step so that the block can be
executed upon completion of the
stance.

This walking technique may be applied to the remaining two knife
hand blocks as well.

2

4

5

HIGH BLOCK VARIATION

(1) Begin by cocking your blocking hand across your chest to your opposite shoulder. The variation exists in the positioning of your opposite arm, which is extended downward in front of you with the palm of its fist pointing toward the floor. (2) Execute a high knife hand block while you simultaneously retract your opposite fist palm upward to your lowest rib.

This block is powerful, fast, and commonly used in conjunction with a counterattack.

LOW BLOCK VARIATION

(1) Begin by cocking your blocking hand across your chest to your opposite shoulder. The variation exists in extending your opposite arm downward in front of you with the palm of its fist pointing toward the floor. (2) Execute a low knife hand block while you simultaneously retract your opposite fist palm upward to your lowest rib.

KNIFE HAND STRIKE (Sohn-Nal-Chi-Ki)

The knife hand strike may be delivered either palm upward or palm downward. For a palm upward strike: (1) Hold your striking hand to the outside, being sure that your elbow is level with your shoulder and your forearm is at a 90-degree angle to the floor. Your opposite arm should be extended downward in front of you with the palm of its fist downward. (2) Step into a back stance or front stance while you simultaneously execute a knife hand palm upward strike

and retract your opposite fist to your lowest rib.

For a palm downward strike: (A) Cock your striking hand across your chest to your opposite shoulder with the palm inward. Your opposite arm should be extended downward in front of you with the palm of its fist pointing toward the floor. (B) Step into a front stance or back stance and simultaneously execute a knife hand palm upward strike. Be sure to retract your opposite fist to your lowest rib at the same time.

WALKING
KNIFE HAND STRIKE

(1) Begin by assuming a ready stance.
(2 & 3) Slide your left foot forward
into a left front stance and simultaneously execute a left knife hand
strike. (4 & 5) Slide your right foot
past your left into a right front
stance and simultaneously execute a
right knife hand strike. Be sure to
cock your striking arm during the
step so that you may execute the
strike upon completion of the turn.
This technique may also be practiced
with the walking back stance. Practice going forward with alternate
steps and strikes, and then practice
moving backward.

1

3

2

4

5

SPEAR HAND THRUST (Pyun-Sohn-Koot-Ji-Lu-Ki)

The spear hand thrust may be delivered either vertically or horizontally. For a vertical spear hand thrust: (1) Begin stepping forward while you cock your striking hand at your side, even with your lowest rib and palm upward. Your opposite hand should be held across your abdomen, palm downward. (2) Thrust your striking hand forward, twisting your wrist to a vertical position with the palm on the inside as you step into a front stance. Upon contact, your arm should be extended. Your opposite hand should protect

your abdomen, palm downward, with the fingertips directly below the elbow of your striking arm. The heel of your opposite palm should be used as the blocking surface.

For a horizontal spear hand thrust: (A) Begin stepping forward while you cock your striking hand at your lowest rib, palm upward. Your opposite hand should execute an outside middle block. (B) Thrust your striking hand forward, twisting your wrist to a horizontal position and thrust it palm downward into the throat, or (C) palm upward into the solar plexus.

WALKING
SPEAR HAND THRUST

(1) Begin by assuming a ready stance.
(2) Begin sliding your left foot forward while you hold both spear hands to waist level at your sides. (3 & 4) Complete the step achieving a left front stance, and simultaneously execute a left vertical spear hand thrust. (5 & 6) Slide your right foot past your left into a right front stance and simultaneously execute a right vertical spear hand thrust.

Practice walking forward with alternate steps, making use of both vertical and horizontal spear hand thrusts.

2

3

5

6

KICKING TECHNIQUES
(Cha-Ki)

Kicking is not a popular means of attack in Western culture, but the leg is considerably more powerful than the arm and also has greater range. Properly applied, a kick can deliver a more devastating blow and in this way provides a distinct advantage over the use of arms.

Balance is an important ingredient in delivering a perfect kick. The supporting leg must be firm enough to support the kick, yet flexible enough to absorb the shock. The foot of the supporting leg is usually flat on the floor with the knee slightly bent. The upper part of the body usually leans in the direction of the kick, although it will have to lean in the opposite direction with such kicks as the side and back kick.

There are four basic kicks, the front kick, the round kick, the side kick and the back kick. Most of the more complex kicks are derived from one of these basics. Thus it is important for a beginner to completely master these basic kicks before going on to their variations.

Any one of these kicks can be executed through one of the following three methods:

THE RISING KICK

This method is executed with the knee locked, instep down and toes up. Its purpose is to limber the leg in order to reach a higher level.

THE SNAP KICK

This method requires speed and rests mostly in knee movement. Its purpose is to attack and withdraw quickly in order to prepare for a second attack or combination of attacks.

THE THRUST KICK

This method places emphasis on power and requires the development of strength. It makes use of both the hip and knee in order to break techniques and reach a target at greater distances.

The striking surfaces of your feet differ from kick to kick. The ball of the foot or the instep is used in the front and round kicks, the outer edge is used in the side kick and the heel is used in the back kick. All kicks can be executed from either front, back or horseback stances.

FRONT KICK
(Ap-Cha-Ki)

(1) Begin by assuming a front stance (although a back or horseback stance may also be substituted). (2) Raise your kicking leg (the rear leg in this case) so that your thigh is parallel to the floor and point your knee at the target. The arch of your foot should be pointing down while your toes are drawn back. The knee of your stationary leg should be slightly bent. (3) Extend and lock your kicking leg straight forward from the knee, keeping your arch down, your instep tensed and your toes drawn back. Make contact with the ball of your foot, and thrust your hip forward with the kick for greater power while maintaining balance with your other leg. (4 & 5) Return your leg to the floor along the same route used to execute the kick.

Practice this kick and all others step-by-step before smoothing your technique into one continuous motion. Following this, you may practice this technique from the walking stances.

2

3

APPLICATION

ROUND KICK
(Dol-Rio-Cha-Ki)

(1) Begin by assuming a back stance (although other stances may be substituted). (2) Raise your kicking leg to the side of your body with the thigh parallel to the floor and at a 90-degree angle to your stationary foot. Your instep should be tensed and your toes drawn back while your chest faces the target. (3) Pivot on the ball of your stationary foot with the direction of your kicking foot until your kicking knee points to the target. From here, extend your kicking leg from the knee, striking the target with the ball of your foot while you continue to roll your hips with the kick for power. Your stationary leg should be bent slightly at the knee with its toes pointing away from the target. (4 & 5) Return your kicking leg to the floor along the same route used to execute the kick.

1

3

4

2

5

INSTEP FRONT KICK

This technique is executed in exactly the same way as the standard front kick, except your toes are pointed downward upon delivery, making the instep (or top part of your foot) the striking surface. This variation is most often applied to kicks aimed at the groin, as seen in the application.

INSTEP ROUND KICK

(1) Begin by assuming a back stance. (2) Raise your kicking leg so that its knee points at the target while you simultaneously pivot on the ball of your stationary foot to twist your hips with the kick. (3) Extend your kicking leg from the knee while you continue to turn your hips and strike the target with your instep. (4) Return your kicking leg to the floor along the same route used to execute the kick.

The ball of your foot can be used to strike instead of the instep as pictured.

The advantage of the instep kick is to hit a target at a greater distance.

107

SIDE KICK
(Yop-Cha-Ki)

(1) Begin by assuming a back stance (although other stances may be substituted). (2) Raise your kicking leg until its thigh is parallel to the floor and your foot is level with your stationary knee. Be sure to turn your arch inward and draw your toes back. Your stationary foot should simultaneously pivot to the outside, away from the target. (3) Extend your kicking leg to the target from the knee and make contact with the outside blade of your foot. Lean your upper body towards the target and lock the knee of your stationary leg. (4 & 5) Return your kicking leg to the floor along the same route used to execute the kick.

2

5

SIDE KICK VARIATION

(1) Begin by assuming a back stance (although other stances may be substituted). (2) Raise your kicking leg so that the knee points to the target with your thigh parallel to the floor. (3) Extend your kicking leg to the target from the knee, making contact with the outside blade of your foot, and be sure to simultaneously pivot on your stationary leg. Your body should lean slightly backward during the execution. (4 & 5) Return your kicking foot to the floor along the same route used to execute the kick.

2

4

5

SIDE KICK
IN HORSEBACK STANCE

(1) Begin by assuming a horseback stance with your face turned toward the target. (2) Slide the leg furthest from the target across and in front of your kicking foot. (3) Shift your weight to the foot moved in the previous step and raise your kicking foot until it is level with your stationary knee and the thigh is parallel to the floor. (4) Execute a side kick, turning your hips in the direction of the kick and pivoting your stationary foot away from the target. Be sure to lean your body away from the target as well.

2

4

BACK KICK
(Dwi-Cha-Ki)

(1) Begin in a ready stance and turn your head toward the target, looking over the shoulder on the same side as your kicking leg. (2) Lift your kicking leg until your thigh is parallel to the floor at waist level (or higher) with your foot turned so that its heel faces the target. (3) Thrust your entire kicking leg toward the target from your hip, using the bottom of your heel as the striking surface. Simultaneously twist your hip into the kick to produce power and bend your upper body down away from the target. (4 & 5) Return your kicking leg to the floor along the same route used to execute the kick.

2

4

5

HAND POSITION WHILE KICKING IN BACK STANCE

(1) Assume a ready stance. (2) As your left foot slides forward, pull your right fist back to your lowest rib, palm downward, and cock your left fist across your chest, palm inward. Twist your upper body in the direction both fists have moved. (3) As you slide into a left back stance, snap your left fist in front of you, palm downward, and your right fist to your abdomen, palm inward. Your left forearm should be positioned 45 degrees to the floor with its fist level with your shoulder.

Upon completion of the kick, repeat these hand motions in reverse order to return to your original position.

HAND POSITION WHILE KICKING IN FRONT STANCE

(1) Assume a ready stance. (2) As your left foot slides forward, cross both arms in front of your chest, fists pointing downward. (3) As you slide into a left front stance, snap both fists out to your sides, locking your elbows and turning your palms inward.

Upon completion of the kick, reverse the hand motions to return to your original position.

HAND POSITION
WHILE KICKING IN
HORSEBACK STANCE

(1) Begin by assuming a ready stance. (2) As your left foot begins to slide forward, simultaneously cross both arms in front of your chest. (3 & 4) As your foot completes its forward slide into a horseback stance, simultaneously snap both fists to your sides at hip level and palm inward. Your hands should be two fists distance from your hips and your elbows should be locked.

Following this hand maneuver, the desired kick is executed. Upon completion of the kick, repeat these hand motions in reverse order to return to your original position.

NOTE: Most of these basic kicks are practiced with a walking front stance. However, it is recommended that the round kick be practiced with a walking back stance and the side kick with either a walking back stance or a walking horseback stance.

ELBOW STRIKES
(Pal-Kup-Chi-Ki)

The elbow strike is a very powerful and effective technique at close range since it is so easily controlled and executed. Its primary targets usually include the face, throat, ribs or solar plexus, and its striking surface is the entire elbow area.

FORWARD ELBOW STRIKE

(1) As your opponent attempts a punch, a-chieve a back stance and block it outward, keeping your striking fist palm upward at your lowest rib. (2) Lean forward into a front stance while you simultaneously snap your elbow upward to make contact with your opponent's chin. Be sure that your fist is palm downward at the point of contact.

BACKWARD ELBOW STRIKE

As your opponent attempts to attack you from the rear, snap your elbow upward behind you, being sure to look at your target over the shoulder of your striking arm. Your fist should be clenched with its palm upward.

INSIDE FORWARD ELBOW STRIKE

As your opponent attempts to attack from the front, begin moving your striking arm from its preliminary position (fist clenched, palm up at your lowest rib), twisting your palm downward as you circle your elbow to the target.

SIDE
ELBOW STRIKE

(1) Maintaining a horseback stance, turn your head to your opponent and cock your striking arm across your chest so that your fist is palm inward near your opposite shoulder. (2) Twist your fist palm downward as you thrust your elbow outward in an arc toward the target.

DEFENSE AND REVERSE PUNCHES

Defense and counterattack make common use of the reverse punch in sparring. It can be used with all of the previously explained blocks quite easily and effectively.

When a reverse punch is used following a block in the front stance, simply execute a reverse snap or thrust punch without shifting your balance. When a reverse thrust punch follows a block in the back stance, your weight should shift forward into a front stance. When delivering a reverse snap punch from the back stance, shift your weight slightly forward but maintain the back stance.

Much of the power in striking and blocking is derived from the snapping of your hips and the shifting of your body weight forward. Thus, it is necessary to practice these techniques using that forward snap of your hip.

Examples of defense and reverse punch combinations are as follows:

LOW BLOCK—REVERSE PUNCH

(1) Begin in a left back stance and execute a left low block. (2) Shift your weight forward into a left front stance and simultaneously execute a right reverse punch while you retract your left fist.

HIGH BLOCK—REVERSE PUNCH

(1) Begin in a left back stance and execute a left high block. (2) Shift your weight forward into a left front stance and simultaneously execute a right reverse punch while you retract your left fist.

OUTSIDE MIDDLE BLOCK—REVERSE PUNCH

(1) Begin in a left back stance and execute a left outside middle block. (2) Shift your weight forward into a front stance and simultaneously execute a right reverse punch while you retract your left fist.

INSIDE MIDDLE BLOCK—REVERSE PUNCH

(1) Begin in a left back stance and execute a left inside middle block. (2) Shift your weight forward into a left front stance while you simultaneously execute a right reverse punch and retract your left fist.

KNIFE HAND BLOCK—REVERSE PUNCH

(1) Begin in a left back stance and execute a left knife hand block (In this instance, you should keep your right fist retracted). (2) Shift your weight forward into a left front stance and simultaneously execute a right reverse punch while you retract your left fist.

SPARRING TECHNIQUES
(Kyo-Lu-Ki)

There are four different stages to learning sparring techniques. They are: three-step sparring, one-step sparring, prearranged free sparring and free sparring. The basic forms of the first two stages will be outlined in detail. In the third stage, prearranged free sparring (Ma-Chu-O-Kyoluki), you and your partner will apply the techniques you learned in the previous two stages and rearrange the pattern of attack and choice of techniques to suit yourselves. During prearranged free sparring, the attacker should apply a combination of techniques, while the defender learns the application of blocking techniques, moving swiftly to avoid an attack and making use of proper counterattacks.

The final stage, free sparring (Kyo-Lu-Ki), is the most important and difficult since it simulates actual combat and makes use of all offensive and defensive techniques previously learned. Remain relaxed while sparring and maintain your flexibility, reflexes and stamina. A degree of mental confidence is also necessary in order to understand the pattern of attack in each case and overcome it.

Since prearranged sparring and free sparring techniques depend solely upon the individuals involved, showing examples of their usage would be defeating the purpose of student initiative and reflexive training. However, you should be sure to make use of all techniques and basics previously offered in this book during your free sparring sessions.

It is important to note that contact is not permitted in any of these stages, since good technique and control requires you to focus your blows one inch away from the target.

THREE-STEP SPARRING
(Se-Bon-Kyoluki)

The attacker should advance three times with a punch or kick, while the defender blocks three times in moving backward and then counter-attack. This will train you to block effectively, develop coordination and balance, and practice your counter-attacking techniques.

(1) Begin by assuming a ready stance and bow to your partner. (2) The attacker (**A,** on the left) steps forward into a left front stance and simultaneously executes a left low block. (3) As **A** steps forward into a right front stance and attempts a right high punch, the defender (**B,** on

the right) steps back with his right foot into a left front stance and executes a left high block. (4) **A** steps forward into a left front stance and attempts a left high punch while **B** steps his left foot back into a right front stance and executes a right high block. (5) **A** steps forward into a right front stance and attempts a right high punch while **B** steps his right foot back into a left back stance and executes a left high block. (6) **B** immediately executes a right front kick to **A's** abdomen. (7) **B** drops his kicking leg to the floor to achieve a right back stance and executes a right knife hand strike to **A's** temple.

ONE-STEP SPARRING (I) (Han-Bon-Kyoluki)

The attacker should advance once with a punch or kick, while the defender blocks the attack by moving either forward or backward. This form of sparring requires more flexibility and determination in blocking and attacking. It also requires quicker movement in either direction into a position of counterattack.

(1) Following the ceremonial opening (i.e., ready stance and bow) the attacker (**A,** on the left) steps forward into a left front stance and executes a left low block. (2) **A** attempts a right front kick while the defender (**B,** on the right) steps forward with his right foot into a right back stance and executes a right low block. (3) **B** shifts his weight to achieve a right front stance and executes a left reverse punch to **A's** kidney.

ONE-STEP SPARRING
(II)

(1) Following the ceremonial opening (i.e., ready stance and bow), the attacker (**A,** on the left) steps forward into a left front stance and executes a left low block. (2) **A** steps forward into a right front stance and attempts a right middle punch while the defender (**B,** on the right) steps his right foot forward into a right back stance and executes a right inside middle block. (3) **B** pivots on the balls of both feet into a horseback stance and executes a right elbow strike to **A's** solar plexus while simultaneously grasping **A's** extended arm with his left hand. (4) Maintaining his grasp and stance, **B** executes a right back knuckle strike to **A's** face.

133

ONE-STEP SPARRING
(III)

(1) Following the ceremonial opening, **A** steps into a left front stance and executes a left low block. (2) **A** steps his right foot forward into a right front stance and attempts a right middle punch while **B** steps into a right back stance and executes a right knife hand block. (3) **B** executes a side kick to **A's** armpit. (4) **B** returns his right leg to the floor near his left leg and executes a left roundhouse kick to **A's** ribs while maintaining a grasp of **A's** extended arm.

ONE-STEP SPARRING (IV)

(1) Following the ceremonial opening **A** begins his attack by (2) stepping into a horseback stance and attempting a left high punch. **B** steps into a right back stance and executes a right high block. (3) Maintaining his high block posture, **B** shifts his weight into a right front stance and executes a left reverse punch to **A's** solar plexus.

ONE-STEP SPARRING (V)

(1) Following the ceremonial opening, **A** steps into a left front stance and attempts a left reverse punch while **B** steps into a right back stance and executes outside middle block. (2) Maintaining his block, **B** shifts his weight to achieve a right front stance and executes a left knife hand strike (palm up) to **A's** neck.

ONE-STEP SPARRING (VI)

(1) Following the ceremonial opening, **A** steps into a right front stance and attempts a left reverse punch while **B** steps back into a right back stance and executes an inside middle block. (2) Maintaining his middle block, **B** shifts his weight into a right front stance and executes a left reverse punch to **A's** face.

SELF-DEFENSE TECHNIQUES
(Ho-Sin-Sool)

Self-defense techniques are particularly useful for women, and are designed to enable you to break free of various holds and deliver a counterattack, or at least apply a technique to restrain the aggressor. The following pages show a few examples of self-defense techniques for beginners.

SELF-DEFENSE
(I)

(1) An attacker grabs you from behind pinning both arms to your sides. (2) Spread your feet to achieve better balance while you raise your arms to shoulder height (elbows out)

to break the hold. (3) Execute a reverse elbow strike to the attacker's solar plexus. (4) Turn your upper body and deliver a right hook punch to the attacker's face.

SELF-DEFENSE (II)

(1) An attacker grabs you from the front pinning both arms to your sides. (2) Spread your feet to achieve balance and simultaneously raise your arms (elbows out) to break the hold. (3) Deliver two straight punches to the attacker's ribs. (4) Pull the attacker's head downward with your hands while you simultaneously execute an upward knee strike to his face.

SELF-DEFENSE
(III)

(1) An attacker grabs you by the right wrist. (2) Pivot on the ball of your left foot while you deliver a right side kick to the attacker's knee. (3 & 4) Retract your kicking leg to the ground near your opposite leg and then execute a left round kick to the attacker's solar plexus.

FORMS
(Poom-Se)

Forms were designed to arrange basic techniques in continuous motion, and were given under the assumption that one is being attacked from all directions. It is important to practice forms with patience and concentration since they are geared to increase your accuracy, balance, coordination, speed and endurance.

Below the black belt level, there are eight *Palgye* forms, eight *Tae Kook* forms and three *Kicho* forms. The Kicho forms and the first three **Palgye** forms will be covered in this book. The remaining forms will be covered in a subsequent volume aimed at the intermediate level.

NOTE: All six forms covered in this book follow the same "I" shaped floor pattern. This pattern is explained in detail for the first form (Kicho No. 1), but can be used as reference for the remaining Kicho and Palgye forms.

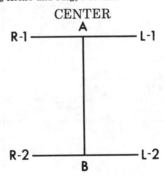

FORMS AT A GLANCE
KICHO IL-BOO No. 1
("I" PATTERN)

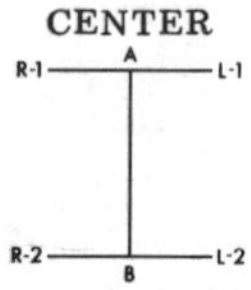

CENTER

R-1 ——— A ——— L-1

R-2 ——— B ——— L-2

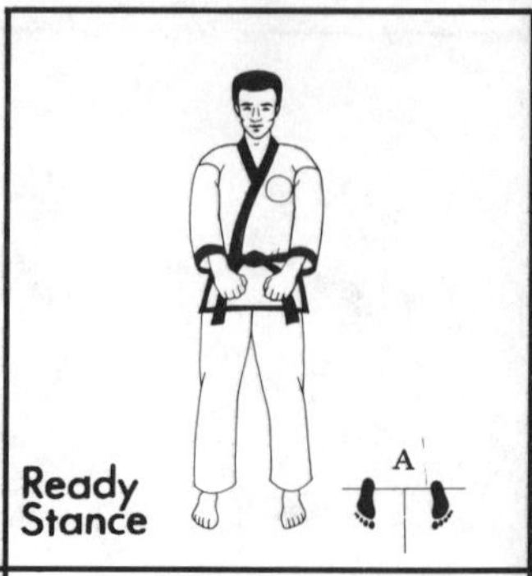

Ready Stance

A

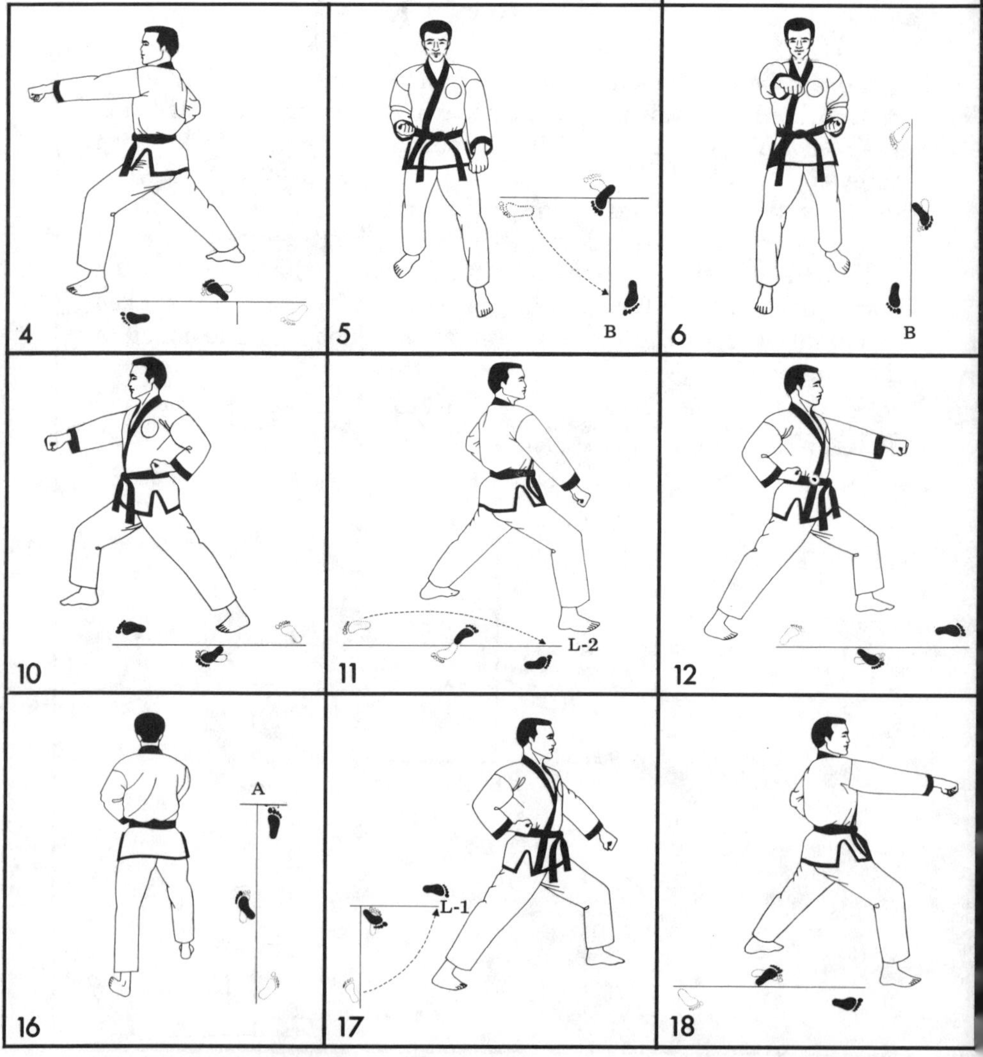

4

5 B

6 B

10

11 L-2

12

16 A

17 L-1

18

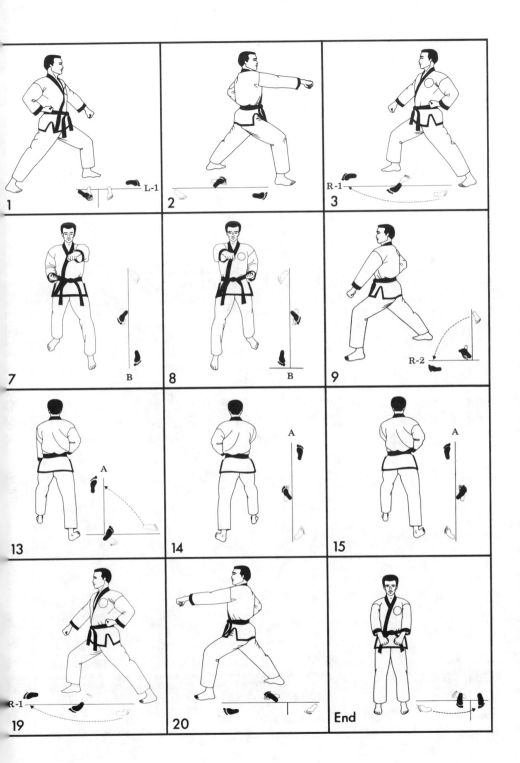

1

2   L-1

3   R-1

7   B

8   B

9   R-2

13   A

14   A

15   A

19   R-1

20

End

KICHO IL-BOO
(No.1)

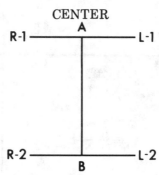

Ready Stance

(Ready Stance) Begin by assuming a ready stance at center (A). (1a & 1) Turn 90 degrees counterclockwise into a left front stance and simul-

1a

taneously execute a left low block. (2a & 2) Slide your right foot past your left to position L-1 to assume a right front stance and simultaneously execute a right middle punch. (3a & 3) Pivoting on your left foot, turn 180 degrees clockwise into a right front stance and simultaneously execute a right low block. (4a & 4) Slide your left foot past your right to position R-1 to assume a left front stance and simultaneously execute a left middle punch. (5a & 5) Pivoting

on your right foot, turn 90 degrees counterclockwise into a left front stance and simultaneously execute a left low block. (6) Slide your right foot past your left into a right front stance and simultaneously execute a right middle punch. (7) Slide your left foot past your right into a left front stance and simultaneously execute a left middle punch. (8) Slide your right foot past your left to position B, assuming a right front stance, and simultaneously execute a right middle punch. Execute *Ki-Up* (shout) with the punch. (9a & 9)

5a

5

7

8

9a

Pivoting on the ball of your right foot, turn your body 270 degrees counterclockwise into a left front stance and simultaneously execute a left low block. (10) Slide your right foot past your left to position R-2, assuming a right front stance, and simultaneously execute a right middle punch. (11a & 11) Pivoting on your left foot, turn your body 180 degrees clockwise to assume a right front stance and simultaneously execute a right low block. (12) Slide

11a

9

10

11

12

13a

your left foot past your right to position L-2, assuming a left front stance, and simultaneously execute a left middle punch. (13a & 13) Pivoting on your right foot, turn your body 90 degrees counterclockwise to assume a left front stance and simultaneously execute a left low block. (14) Slide your right foot past your left into a right front stance and simultaneously execute a right middle punch. (15) Slide your left foot past your right into a left front stance and simultaneously execute a left middle punch. (16) Slide your right foot past your left to position A, assuming a right front stance, and simultaneously execute a right middle punch. Ki-Up with the punch. (17a & 17) Pivoting on the ball of your right foot, turn your body 270 degrees counterclockwise into a left front stance and simultaneously

15

13

14

16

17a

execute a left low block. (18) Slide your right foot past your left to position L-1, assuming a right front stance, and simultaneously execute a right middle punch. (19) Pivoting on your left foot, turn your body 180 degrees clockwise into a right front stance and simultaneously execute a right low block. (20) Slide your left foot past your right into a left front stance and simultaneously execute a left middle punch. (Turn & End) Pivoting on your right foot, turn your body 90 degrees counter-clockwise into a ready stance at center (A).

18

19

Turn

End

159

KICHO EE-BOO
(No.2)

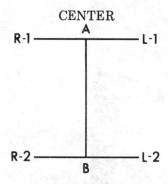

Ready
Stance

(Ready Stance) Begin by assuming a ready stance at center (A). (1) Pivoting on your right foot, turn your body 90 degrees counterclockwise into a left front stance and simultaneously execute a left low block. (2) Slide your right foot past

1

your left, assuming a right front stance, and simultaneously execute a right high punch. (3) Pivoting on your left foot, turn your body 180 degrees clockwise, assuming a right front stance, and simultaneously execute a right low block. (4) Slide your left foot past your right into a left front stance and simultaneously execute a left high punch. (5) Pivoting on your right foot, turn your body 90 degrees counterclockwise, assuming a left front stance, and simultaneously execute a left low block. (6) Slide your right foot past your left into a right front stance and simultaneously execute a right high block. (7) Slide your left foot past your right into a left front stance and simultaneously execute a left high block. (8) Slide your right foot past

3

4

6

7

163

your left into a right front stance and simultaneously execute a right high block. Ki-Up with the block. (9) Pivoting on your right leg, turn your body 270 degrees counterclockwise into a left front stance and simultaneously execute a left low block. (10) Slide your right foot past your left into a right front stance and simultaneously execute a right high punch. (11) Pivoting on your left foot, turn your body 180 degrees clockwise into a right front stance and simultaneously execute a right low block. (12) Slide your left foot past your right to assume a left front stance and simultaneously execute a left high punch. (13) Pivoting on

9

10

12

13

your right foot, turn your body 90 degrees counterclockwise to assume a left front stance and simultaneously execute a left low block. (14) Slide your right foot past your left to assume a right front stance and simultaneously execute a right high block. (15) Slide your left foot past your right to assume a left front stance and simultaneously execute a left high block. (16) Slide your right foot past your left to assume a right front stance and simultaneously execute a right high block. Ki-Up with the block. (17) Pivoting on your right foot, turn your body 270 degrees counterclockwise to assume a left front stance and simultaneously execute a left low block. (18) Slide your right foot past your left into a right front stance and simultaneously execute a right high punch. (19) Pivoting on your left foot, turn your body 180 degrees clockwise to assume a right front stance and simultaneously execute a right low block. (20) Slide your left foot past

14

17

15

16

18

19

20

your right to assume a left front stance and simultaneously execute a left high punch. (End) Pivoting on your right foot, turn your body 90 degrees counterclockwise to assume a ready stance at center (A).

End

KICHO SAM-BOO
(No.3)

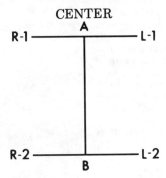

Ready Stance

(Ready Stance) Begin by assuming a ready stance at center (A). (1a & 1) Slide your left foot 90 degrees counterclockwise to assume a left back stance and simultaneously execute a left outside middle block. (2) Slide your right foot past your left into a right front stance and simultaneously execute a right middle punch. (3a & 3) Pivoting on your left foot, turn your body 180 degrees clockwise to assume a right back stance and simultaneously execute a right outside middle block. (4) Slide your

2

1a

1

3a

3

left foot past your right to assume a left front stance and simultaneously execute a left middle punch. (5) Pivoting on your right foot, turn your body 90 degrees counterclockwise to assume a left front stance and simultaneously execute a left low block. (6a & 6) Slide your right foot past your left to assume a horseback stance and simultaneously execute a right side punch. (7) Pivoting on your right foot, turn your body 180 degrees clockwise to assume a horseback stance (your chest facing the opposite direction from the previous step) and simultaneously execute a left side punch. (8) Pivoting on your left foot, turn your body 180 degrees counterclockwise to assume a horseback stance and simultaneously execute a right side punch. Ki-Up with the punch. (9a & 9) Pivoting on your

9

right foot, turn your body 90 degrees counterclockwise to assume a left back stance and simultaneously execute a left outside middle block. (10) Slide your right foot past your left to assume a right front stance and simultaneously execute a right middle punch. (11) Pivoting on your left foot, turn your body 180 degrees clockwise to assume a right back stance and simultaneously execute a right outside middle block. (12) Slide your left foot past your right into a left front stance and simultaneously execute a left middle punch. (13) Pivoting on your right foot, turn your body 90 degrees counterclockwise to assume a left front stance and simultaneously execute a left low block. (14) Slide your right foot past

11

9

10

12

13

14

your left to assume a horseback stance and simultaneously execute a right side punch. (15) Pivoting on your right foot, turn your body 180 degrees clockwise into a horseback stance (chest facing in opposite direction of previous step) and simultaneously execute a left side punch. (16) Pivoting on your left foot, turn your body 180 degrees counterclockwise to assume a horseback stance and simultaneously execute a right side punch. Ki-Up with the punch. (17a & 17) Pivoting on your right foot, slide your left foot 90 degrees counterclockwise to assume a left back stance and simultaneously execute a left outside middle block. (18) Slide your right foot past your left to assume a right front stance and simultaneously execute a right middle punch. (19) Pivoting on your left

17a

15

16

17

18

foot, turn your body 180 degrees clockwise to assume a right back stance and simultaneously execute a right outside middle block. (20) Slide your left foot past your right into a left front stance and simultaneously execute a left middle punch. (End) Pivoting on your right foot, turn your body 90 degrees counterclockwise to assume a ready stance at center (A).

PALGYE IL-CHANG
(No.1)

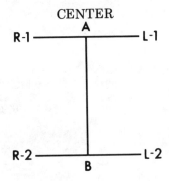

Ready Stance

(Ready Stance) Begin by assuming the ready stance at center (A). (1) Pivoting on your right foot, turn your body 90 degrees counterclockwise to assume a left front stance and simultaneously execute a left low block. (2a & 2) Slide your right foot past your left to assume a right front stance and simultaneously execute a right inside middle block. (3) Pivoting on your left foot, turn your body 180 degrees clockwise to assume a right front stance and simultaneously execute a right low block. (4a & 4) Slide your left foot past your right to assume a left front stance and simul-

2

taneously execute a left inside middle block. (5) Pivoting on your right foot, turn your body 90 degrees counterclockwise to assume a left front stance and simultaneously execute a left low block. (6) Slide your right foot past your left to assume a right back stance and simultaneously execute a right inside middle block. (7) Slide your left foot past your right to assume a left back stance and simultaneously execute a left inside middle block. (8) Slide your right foot past your left to assume a right front stance and simultaneously execute a right middle punch. Ki-Up with the punch. (9) Pivoting on your right foot, turn your body 270 degrees counterclockwise into a left back stance and simultaneously execute a left knife hand middle block. (10) Slide your

right foot past your left to assume a right back stance and simultaneously execute a right inside middle block. (11) Pivoting on your left foot, turn your body 180 degrees clockwise to assume a right back stance and simultaneously execute a right knife hand middle block. (12) Slide your left foot past your right to assume a left back stance and simultaneously execute a left inside middle block. (13) Pivoting on your right foot, turn your body 90 degrees counterclockwise to assume a left front stance and simultaneously execute a left low block. (14) Slide your right foot past your left to assume a right front stance and simultaneously execute a right knife hand strike (palm upward). (15) Slide your left foot past

your right to assume a left front stance and simultaneously execute a left knife hand strike (palm upward). (16) Slide your right foot past your left to assume a right front stance and simultaneously execute a right middle punch. Ki-Up with the punch. (17) Pivoting on your right foot, turn your body 270 degrees counterclockwise to assume a left front stance and simultaneously execute a left low block. (18) Slide your right foot past your left to assume a right front stance and simultaneously execute a right inside middle block. (19) Pivoting on your left foot, turn your body 180 degrees clockwise to assume a right front stance and simultaneously execute a right low block. (20) Slide your left foot past your right to assume a left front stance and simultaneously execute a left inside middle block. (End) Pivoting on your right foot, turn your body 90 degrees counterclockwise to assume a ready stance at center (A).

16

19

17

18

20

End

PALGYE EE-CHANG
(No.2)

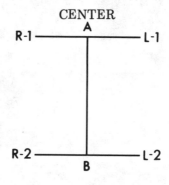

(Ready Stance) Begin by assuming a ready stance at center (A). (1) Pivoting on your right foot, turn your body 90 degrees counterclockwise to assume a left front stance and simultaneously execute a left high block. (2a) Maintaining your high

Ready Stance

1

2a

block posture, execute a right high front kick. (2) Drop your kicking leg to the floor so that you assume a right front stance and simultaneously execute a right middle punch. (3) Pivoting on your left foot, turn your body 180 degrees clockwise to assume a right front stance and simultaneously execute a right high block. (4a) Maintaining your high block posture, execute a high left front kick. (4) Drop your kicking foot to the floor so that you assume a left front stance and simultaneously execute a left middle punch. (5) Pivoting on your right foot, turn your body 90 degrees counterclockwise to assume a left back stance and simultaneously execute a left knife hand low block. (6) Slide your right

4a

2

3

4

5

6

foot past your left to assume a right back stance and simultaneously execute a right knife hand middle block. (7) Slide your left foot past your right to assume a left front stance and simultaneously execute a left high block. (8) Slide your right foot past your left to assume a right front stance and simultaneously execute a right middle punch. Ki-Up with the punch. (9) Pivoting on your right foot, turn your body 270 degrees counterclockwise to assume a left front stance and simultaneously execute a left high block. (10a) Maintaining your high block posture, execute a high right front kick. (10) Drop your kicking foot to the floor so that you assume a right front stance and simultaneously execute a right middle punch. (11) Pivoting on

9

7

8

10a

10

193

11

your left foot, turn your body 180 degrees clockwise to assume a right front stance and simultaneously execute a right high block. (12a) Maintaining your high block posture, execute a high left front kick. (12) Drop your kicking foot to the floor so that you assume a left front stance and simultaneously execute a left middle punch. (13) Pivoting on your right foot, turn your body 90 degrees counterclockwise to assume a left back stance and simultaneously execute a left low block (right hand assisting). (14) Slide your right foot past your left to assume a right back stance and simultaneously execute a right middle block (left hand assisting). (15) Slide your left foot past your right to assume a left back stance and simultaneously execute a left inside middle block. (16) Slide

FRONT VIEW

13

12a

12

FRONT VIEW

14

FRONT VIEW

15

195

16

your right foot past your left to assume a right front stance and simultaneously execute a right middle punch. Ki-Up with the punch. (17) Pivoting on your right foot, turn your body 270 degrees counterclockwise to assume a left front stance and simultaneously execute a left high block. (18a) Maintaining your high block posture, execute a high right front kick. (18) Drop your kicking foot to the floor so that you assume a right front stance and simultaneously execute a right middle punch. (19) Pivoting on your left foot, turn your body 180 degrees clockwise to assume a right front stance and simultaneously execute a right high block. (20a) Maintaining your high block posture, execute a high left front kick. (20) Drop your

18

17

18a

19

20a

197

20

kicking foot to the floor so that you assume a left front stance and simultaneously execute a left middle punch. (End) Pivoting on your right foot, turn your body 90 degrees counterclockwise to assume a ready stance at center (A).

End

PALGYE SAM-CHANG
(No.3)

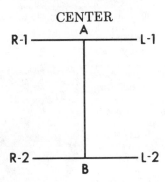

Ready Stance

(Ready Stance) Begin by assuming a ready stance at center (A). (1) Pivoting on your right foot, turn your body 90 degrees counterclockwise to assume a left front stance and simultaneously execute a left low block. (2) Slide your right foot past your left to assume a right front stance and simultaneously execute a right middle punch. (3) Pivoting on your left foot, turn your body 180 degrees clockwise to assume a right front stance and simultaneously execute a right low block. (4) Slide your left foot past your right to assume a left front stance and simultaneously execute a left middle punch. (5) Pivoting on your right foot, turn your body 90 degrees counterclockwise to assume a left front stance and simultaneously execute a left low block. (6) Slide your right foot past

3

6

your left to assume a right front stance and simultaneously execute a right high block. (7) Slide your left foot past your right to assume a left front stance and simultaneously execute a left high block. (8) Slide your right foot past your left to assume a right front stance and simultaneously execute a right high punch. Ki-Up with the punch. (9) Pivoting on your right foot, turn your body 270 degrees counterclockwise to assume a left back stance and simultaneously execute a left knife hand middle block. (10) Slide your right foot past your left to assume a right back stance and simultaneously execute a right middle knife hand block. (11) Pivoting on your left leg, turn your body 180 degrees clockwise to assume a right back stance and simultaneously execute a right middle knife hand block. (12) Slide your

9

7

8

10

11

12

left foot past your right to assume a
left back stance and simultaneously
execute a left knife hand middle
block. (13) Pivoting on your right
foot, turn your body 90 degrees
counterclockwise to assume a left
back stance and simultaneously execute a left outside middle block. (14)
Pivoting on both feet, turn your
body 180 degrees clockwise to
assume a right back stance and
simultaneously execute a right outside middle block. (NOTE: Both of
your feet should merely turn during
this step, each pivoting 90 degrees
clockwise.) (15) Slide your right foot
backward past your left to assume a
left back stance and simultaneously
execute a left inside middle block.
(16) Slide your left foot backward
past your right to assume a right
back stance and simultaneously execute a right inside middle block. (17)
Slide your right foot backward past
your left to assume a left back stance
and simultaneously execute a left
inside middle block. (18) Pivoting on

15

13

14

16

17

both feet, turn your body 180 degrees clockwise to assume a right back stance and simultaneously execute a right outside middle block. (Note: Both of your feet should merely turn during this step, each pivoting 90 degrees clockwise.) (19) Pivoting on your right foot, turn your body 270 degrees counterclockwise to assume a left front stance and simultaneously execute a left high block. (20) Slide your right foot past your left to assume a right front stance and simultaneously execute a right high punch. (21) Pivoting on your left foot, turn your body 180 degrees clockwise to assume a right front stance and simultaneously execute a right high block. (22) Slide your left foot past your right to assume a left front stance and simultaneously execute a left high punch. Ki-Up with the punch. (End) Pivoting on your right foot, turn your body 90 degrees counterclockwise to assume a ready stance at center (A).

19

20

22

End